HOW TO LIVE A PRODUCTIVE LIFE

ANTHONY EKANEM

Copyright © Anthony Ekanem
All Rights Reserved.

This book has been self-published with all reasonable efforts taken to make the material error-free by the author. No part of this book shall be used, reproduced in any manner whatsoever without written permission from the author, except in the case of brief quotations embodied in critical articles and reviews.

The Author of this book is solely responsible and liable for its content including but not limited to the views, representations, descriptions, statements, information, opinions and references ["Content"]. The Content of this book shall not constitute or be construed or deemed to reflect the opinion or expression of the Publisher or Editor. Neither the Publisher nor Editor endorse or approve the Content of this book or guarantee the reliability, accuracy or completeness of the Content published herein and do not make any representations or warranties of any kind, express or implied, including but not limited to the implied warranties of merchantability, fitness for a particular purpose. The Publisher and Editor shall not be liable whatsoever for any errors, omissions, whether such errors or omissions result from negligence, accident, or any other cause or claims for loss or damages of any kind, including without limitation, indirect or consequential loss or damage arising out of use, inability to use, or about the reliability, accuracy or sufficiency of the information contained in this book.

Made with ♥ on the Notion Press Platform
www.notionpress.com

Contents

Preface

Welcome to the digital age. While we take for granted much of the technology that surrounds us and the way it has changed the way we work and relax; it's very important to recognise just how much it has impacted our lives. Today we are constantly bombarded by information and stimulation, and it is taking its toll on our brains. Meanwhile, the expectations placed on us by our work have only increased as a result of greater productivity tools and enhanced connectivity.

And it's not just technology that has changed life for us either. The demands placed on us in other areas have also increased. The world is more populous, living costs have gone up and our roles in society have changed. More and more women are now working full-time, which while a good thing, has created new challenges in trying to raise and care for our children. The roles of men have likewise become increasingly uncertain and competition for employment is fiercer than ever. Don't get me wrong – none of this is bad in itself! Having greater access to entertainment, being able to communicate with anyone in the world and enjoying greater equality than ever before are all good things.

The state of the economy is a little less rosy. But all in all, times are good. The problem? We're having a hard time keeping up with all this change! And it's leading to burnout.

For a great number of us, the demands placed on us are simply too great for us to shoulder. The constant stimulation and bombardment of information are leading to burnout. And knowing how to get what we want from life is seemingly impossible.

Our brains evolved in entirely different environments, and they simply aren't designed to thrive under these conditions. The result is what we call 'overwhelm'. That means too much information, too much pressure, too much to do and too little time. We end up stressed, exhausted and disorganised and it's just not good for our health.

The Modern Dilemma

Perhaps this sounds familiar. You wake up with a jolt first thing in the morning because your alarm has gone off. In a rush, you clean your teeth and get ready for work while watching the news on whichever device you prefer. You pack your family off for school and work respectively and then you set off yourself. You're late because it took you 20 minutes to choose what you were going to wear and to find your keys. And because you lay there on the couch for 5 minutes doing nothing.

What follows is a tedious and frustrating 10-90 minutes of commuting – complete with angry fellow commuters, stuffy carriages and probably a fair amount of time spent playing Candy Crush. By the time you get to work, you're already stressed, late and feeling a headache coming on from peering at a small screen under artificial lighting.

You then have a strong coffee, leaving you feeling wired, and you open your inbox to 10,000 emails (okay, maybe that's an exaggeration but you get the point!). You set yourself some things to achieve for the day – just so you can get back to feeling 'on top' of work, but then you spend the next 20 minutes on Facebook and YouTube watching cat videos. And staring at photos of your friends on sunny holidays wondering what went so wrong with your life.

Lunch comes and you feel like you've barely done anything. You head out for lunch and grab the cheapest thing you can find that's sugary and have another strong coffee. This doesn't exactly fuel you with energy for the second half of the day, which is spent largely putting out fires. How can you be expected to progress in your career and get the kind of lifestyle you want, when you're spending all your time treading water? By the end of the day, you've spent most of your time responding to emails and trying not to get distracted. You end up leaving an hour late, which is followed by another hour of commuting.

You're now home at 7 PM. You should make a healthy meal for your family, maybe suggest a fun activity that you can all get up to? But you're completely stuck for inspiration, so instead, you put on a pizza and a film and crash on the couch for the next hour. The house is untidy and messy though, so you feel generally anxious and stressed instead of getting any relaxation.

There were things you were meant to do this evening too: calling your friend whom you haven't spoken to in ages for example was high on the list. So was paying that bill. Only you can't face the idea of paying that bill because you don't want to rummage through the piles of documents on your desk. You're not even sure you can find the bill anymore. Which would mean calling them on your lunch break to get them to send out another one.

You haven't even looked at your bank account because you don't want to know how bad it is. You're supposed to be saving for a mortgage or your child's college fund, but you have that party coming up that you can't afford but can't get out of either. And you don't want to call your friend because you've now only got an hour left before you start getting ready for bed. And how can you justify calling that friend when you haven't paid the bill? So you avoid looking at the WhatsApp message because you don't want them to see that you've seen it. Let alone spending any time with your wife/husband?

Then you get an email from work reminding you how much you have to do tomorrow, which only stressed you out further. You browse Facebook a bit more and respond to some notifications from Candy Crush. Then you hit the sack – later than planned – and having done barely any of the things you wanted to do. You still haven't read that new book you bought and were excited about.

Maybe tomorrow will be a better day? Except you can't get any sleep because you're stressed and you just spent the last hours before bed looking at screens. And the coffee is still in your system. And at the weekend you have about 20 things to do and that dinner party you're supposed to be going to.

Conquering Information Overload

That last section wasn't designed to make you feel even more stressed and anxious than perhaps you already are. Rather, it was intended to draw attention to some of the very real issues that we face daily. Most of us simply have too much to do, we are too 'wired' and we are too bombarded with information, decisions and more. Approximately half of us are burned out because we're trying to do too much and struggling to keep afloat. The irony is that we end up achieving less the more we try and squeeze in and as such, we can never get ahead.

But there is an answer and there are ways around these problems. The secret is organization. It might sound like a small thing but staying organised is everything in today's environment. By staying organised and keeping on top of all that information, those huge to-do lists and your calendar, you can take each challenge one step at a time.

You can automate some of the work that is taking up the most time and energy, you can delegate and you can find better ways to think about the problems and challenges that come up. Once you learn to prioritize, organise and schedule, you'll find life becomes much more manageable and that you have far more time for yourself, your family and your goals. You get to enjoy life again, while at the same time standing more of a chance of achieving everything you want to achieve.

The digital age is partly the result of all the computers and tools that are now integral to the way we work. So, the solution? Start thinking and working more like a computer. That means being methodical, organised, and logical. You'll learn all this and much more in this book.

Specifically, you will learn:

- How to reduce the number of decisions you have to make in a day
- How to prioritize the most important tasks
- How to schedule rest and recovery
- How to save time by delegating and automating your tasks
- How to keep your home more organised
- How to calm your mind to eliminate stress
- How to work more efficiently
- How to reduce notifications while still staying connected
- How to organise your thoughts
- How to create systems, to-do lists and filing methods to help you stay on top of your work
- And much more!

By the end, you'll have organised your life so that you can again feel 'on top' of everything and start making real progress. The best bit? This is all stuff you can do right now. Instead of battling through the stress and hoping one day life will get better, you're instead implementing simple changes right now that can make all the difference.

For the very best results, I recommend taking a single day off from work and cancelling all your other commitments. You're then going to use this one day to work through all your small tasks, to implement new systems, to tidy up and generally to give yourself that 'refresh' that you so desperately need.

This is how you live a productive life. And once your mind is organised, everything else starts falling into place. You'll be more disciplined, more productive, happier, more efficient and less stressed.

CHAPTER ONE

Too Many Decisions

A great place to start is to remove those difficult decisions that are taking up our 'mental bandwidth'. Many of us think that the big 'limit' on our ability to get things done is time. We all make the excuse that we don't exercise because we don't have time and that we don't do more with the family because we don't have time. That's not true. If you think back to all of those times in your life when you've been doing 'nothing', then you'll probably realize that you had plenty of time. Just this week, you've probably spent at least a good couple of hours on Facebook/YouTube/the website of your choice, and there's a good chance you've watched a fair amount of useless TV as well. That's all time that you could have been using to exercise, to phone friends, to tidy the house.

The point? You don't have any problem with time. Your problem is with energy. The reason you're not using that available time more efficiently, or even to have fun is that you're low on energy. And did you know that your willpower decreases too as you run out of energy? Not only do you have less physical energy to get up and tidy when you're tired, but you also have less mental willpower to encourage yourself to do it. Energy management then is much more important than time management very often.

And a BIG component of energy management is understanding the impact that decision-making has on our energy levels.

Every time you must make a decision, this takes a toll on your energy levels and leaves you with a little less energy to 'spend' on other tasks. For instance, when you wake up in the morning and decide what you're going to wear, that will not only take up time, but it will also take up energy. Likewise, when you decide what to have for lunch, you'll also be using up your mental energy to make that decision. And this then means that you have less energy when it comes to making other, more important decisions. When someone asks you what to do at work, or when you're wondering how best to save your money, you now have less mental energy available to dedicate to that decision. By the end of the day, you burn out!

How to Reduce Decisions

So, what's the solution? There are many things you can do but one of the most important steps is simply to reduce the number of decisions that you're forced to make in a day. This is something that Steve Jobs is famous for doing. Jobs decided he wanted to reduce the number of trivial decisions he had to make in his life and so he removed all variation from his clothing. He replaced all of his items of clothing with just black t-shirts and jeans. That meant that every single morning, he would put on his one outfit and never need to worry about what he was going to wear! Steve Jobs as you know, would go on to help invent the iPod, iPhone, and iPad. So presumably it was working for him! That's quite extreme of course and not everyone is going to want to surrender all variation in their clothing. Thus, let's look at some more gentle and moderate solutions you can apply to your own life.

Clothing

While you might not want to go as far as Jobs with it, there are nevertheless effective ways you can reduce the decision-making surrounding your choice of outfits. One of the easiest ways to do this is just to plan your outfits so that you have all of those items ready to go. You can even write this out on Sunday evening so you can refer to that plan. This is one of those ideas that sounds perfect in theory but sometimes falls in practice – what happens if you put on that outfit and you don't like it or you're not in the mood for it for instance?

Another solution then is simply to have, say, 20 outfits for work that you know you like and that you know are suitable. Now, you can simply refer to any of those 20 in the morning without too much thought. 20 is enough that your colleagues will only see you in the same outfit once every two months – but you will still never be stressed about whether your outfit works, or because you have nothing to wear.

Another tip is to ensure that you choose your clothes in such a way that they can be combined into multiple different outfits. In other words, make sure that most of your trousers go with most of your tops. Now you'll be able to throw multiple combinations together with less thought.

Food

While you might not want to keep your outfits the same every day, you might well be more inclined to keep your food consistent for breakfast and lunch. These meals aren't exactly 'exciting' in the first place. So why not have the same cereal and toast for breakfast each day and the same salad bar/lunch box for lunch? This reduces waste too, makes shopping much easier and makes it considerably easier to monitor your calorie intake if you're dieting.

As for dinner, this is something else you can plan at the start of the week. And it works even better if you can also prepare some meals – cook something big on Sunday and you can put some Tupperware boxes in the fridge for lazy evenings. Now you can simply heat those meals in the evening instead of throwing a pizza in the oven. And while you're at it, come up with some 'backup' meals that will keep. A good example is to keep a tin of beans in the cupboard. Beans on toast are quite healthy and tasty and they only take 10 minutes to make.

Shopping

If you automate a lot of what you eat, this then creates the opportunity to make your shopping considerably easier. How? By setting up a delivery with your local supermarket. Most stores now offer this service and it means that you can avoid that stressful 'weekly shop' and instead just pick up a few supplementary ingredients to make each of your meals.

'Nights'

You can also schedule some of your daily activities to further reduce decision fatigue. Do this by making each night of the week 'something night'. So now, Monday can become 'rest night' where you're allowed to watch trashy TV without the guilt. Tuesday can become 'date night' where you commit yourself to spending some quality time with your other half. Wednesday can become 'chores night' where you tidy the house. By setting tasks like this for each evening, you remove the stressful need to make that 'right decision' and instead just carry out and execute your plan to stay on top of things. All this will help you to simplify your life. There are more methods you can use to do this as well, so start putting them into action and just reduce the number of decisions you must make.

CHAPTER TWO

Organising Your Home

Now you have some systems in place, you should find a little bit of time and energy freeing up in your day. Maybe you have a slight bit more energy in the evenings and maybe you are a little less stressed on the way to work. The next thing to do is to tidy your home. This is crucial because a tidy home is a reflection of a tidy mind. More than that though, it can also create a tidy mind and here the correlation becomes 'two way'. Not only does a tidy home make it easier to find things, thereby saving time and stress as you're no longer hunting for keys, but it also makes your space that much easier to relax in. Our brains crave order and organization and this is why we find things like tilted picture frames so distressing.

When your home is tidy, you'll have a calming space you can use to relax. What's more, you'll have the confidence of knowing where everything is and being able to retrieve it as and when you need it and fewer occasions when you need to hunt for lost items. So how do you start putting this into action?

Get Ruthless

One of the single most important things you can do to make your home tidier and easier to get around is to get ruthless and start throwing things out.

This sounds ruthless and at first, you might object to the idea of parting with your possessions. Though, reducing your items can make your home considerably less stressful and help you to stay on top of your chores a lot more easily. A good place to start is with your ornaments and knick-knacks. Go through all the things you have on display on your sides and throw out half of those items – or at least put them away somewhere.

By doing this, you have now created a much more minimal space, which is immediately going to feel less stressful to spend time in. At the same time though, you've also created less work for yourself – you now have surfaces you can very easily clean by wiping a cloth around instead of needing to first remove all your items individually. And on top of all that, you have increased the average quality of the things on display. What's left behind will now be only your very favourite things. That means that those favourite items will get much more attention and focus, versus all those other things that were detracting from them.

Another way to be more ruthless is to find all the boxes under your bed and in your wardrobe that you haven't been in for the last 6 months. Remove anything valuable or sentimental and throw the rest out. If you haven't used it in all this time, then you don't need it! What you'll find is that you surprisingly don't miss any of those items and if you find that you suddenly need a mini torch, or whatever else it was, then you can simply buy a new one!

Designated Rooms

Another thing to do is to try and create more separation between your rooms and to think about how they'll affect you unconsciously. For instance, if you currently iron in your living room or your bedroom, you're making it harder to relax in that space. Why? Because now you associate those rooms with work. What's more is that you'll probably have piles of un-ironed clothes in the rooms and clothes on horses.

Better is to make one of the spare rooms in your home your 'chores' room. That way, if that room becomes untidy, then it won't spill out into the other rooms of your home. Alternatively, if you have children and a dog and you find that keeping your home tidy is an uphill struggle, then try keeping just one room in your hoes sacred. Let this be the room where you come to unwind with a book and make some rules that will help it to stay completely pristine: no food, no ironing, no chores etc.

Staying on Top of Cleaning

The tip that we all know very well when it comes to keeping the house clean is to wash up as you go, rather than letting your washing up build-up. This is a good tip but if it's something you've never managed to stick to, then there are a few things you can do to make it easier. One tip is to reduce the amount of crockery you have. You only need enough crockery to entertain the maximum number of guests you have. Above that and you just give yourself an excuse to keep reusing plates and dishes rather than washing them. If there's nothing to eat off of, then you'll be forced to stay tidy.

If you're struggling to stay tidy and if you're a young professional, then consider getting paper plates. You can get a large number of paper plates for very little and if you eat off of these, you can just throw them out each time you're done. Generally, one of the best tips for staying on top of your cleaning is to automate and outsource. If you have the money, then hiring a cleaner will be one of the best investments you ever make. Otherwise, though, think about the technology that can help. Getting a dishwasher for instance will make it MUCH easier to stay on top of washing up as there will only be a few things that you can't put in there. Likewise, you can look into many other devices to help you keep things clean:

- A small portable vacuum cleaner makes vacuuming much easier than a heavy one you have to empty
- A robotic vacuum cleaner can make life even easier!
- A steamer can make ironing less of a chore
- A washing machine and drier are a must

Think about how easy it is to wash things up when you buy them. It's very easy to say you're going to use that smoothie regularly until you've tried washing those blades! There are smoothie models though that are designed specifically to remove this challenge, so that might be a better choice. Likewise, a colander is much easier to wash than a sieve.

Aim High

Finally, make sure that you aim high when it comes to your property. When many of us imagine what we want life to be like once we're highly successful, we will often picture ourselves living in beautiful homes. This should give you just some idea as to how important a good home is to our happiness and sense of accomplishment. The tips above will help you to make a much tidier home and thus nicer to spend time in, but there are other things you can do as well to make your property more similar to the kind of place you dream of living.

For example, you'd be surprised at the things you can buy cheaply that will give your home a unique look or even more functionality. For example, you can make your home into a 'smart home' for much less than you probably expect.

Coloured bulbs with controllers, for instance, are available from Amazon for as little as a few dollars. Likewise, a cheap fountain can make all the difference to your conservatory. There are some very funky Bluetooth speakers you can get cheaply too to create your surround sound.

Take real pride in your home and look at ways to make it a relaxing and comforting experience for less. If you have the money you can go much further and do things like installing a home sauna. This might seem expensive but the difference that a beautiful home can make to your mental state is huge. This is very much worth that extra expense.

CHAPTER THREE

Organising Your Social Life

Do ever feel like life would be a whole lot less stressful if it weren't for all the other people? We all feel like this from time to time – and especially when life is getting on top of us, and we don't have the time, energy or money to devote to our friends. So how do you go about organizing your social life and staying on top of all those things you need to do?

Prioritize

The first thing you need to do is to prioritize. If you have a busy social calendar, then it's often easy to feel overly stressed and put upon. You're constantly being asked out to events and if you say no, then you feel as though you're letting people down. This gets harder and harder as we get older. People move away and meanwhile, we have more and more responsibilities. We feel like we can't say no to a friend who invites us out because it was so long since we saw them last time.

Here's the thing though: there comes a time in life when you just can't do everything you want to do. As such, you need to prioritize and as sad as that sounds, that can sometimes mean pruning your social network. Right at the top of your priorities if you're an adult, should be your partner, your children and your immediate family. If you're having a hard time turning down invitations, then simply remind yourself that you need to reserve the lion's share of your time and energy for your family. This doesn't make you a bad person, it makes you an adult with responsibilities!

This doesn't mean that you're going to cut off contact with your friends or tell them you don't want to see them anymore! All it means is that you might – for example – only accept one invitation to spend time with friends a week. Or more realistically, two a month as you start to get older. That means that if you have two invitations from two sets of friends, you might simply have to decide which friend is one of your 'priorities'.

'Dunbar's Number' is the number of friends that we can realistically maintain relationships with. He puts the number somewhere between 100 - 250, with '150' being the most commonly quoted figure. This number though is not exclusively referring to friends though but rather all the contacts we can maintain whether they be friends, colleagues, associates or acquaintances. In reality, you can probably only maintain about 10 truly close relationships – so choose whom those ten are going to be!

Forget Frenemies

One thing that makes this a lot easier is to think about all the friends you have that aren't friends. These are the people whom we count as friends but whom we don't enjoy spending time around all that much. These are the friends who we constantly moan about to our other friends. And these are the friends who let us down.

As you get older and the stakes get higher, you unfortunately just don't have time for friends who aren't friends. As such, it's time to put those people to one side and focus on the ones whom you enjoy spending time with and who are there for you. Just as removing some of the unnecessary items from your decorating can help to put more emphasis on your favourite belongings, you can likewise enjoy closer relationships with the people who matter to you by spending less time with the people who don't deserve your time and energy.

Keep a Calendar

Another important tip is to keep a calendar. If you have lots of friends and a busy social life, then this is likely to result in a lot of different things planned. One of the biggest stresses that can come from this is being double booked for multiple activities which means letting people down or rushing to try and accomplish both. Keeping a diary is a great way to avoid this from happening and especially if you can use an app that will let you easily update and edit events on the fly. This way you can also set up different reminders to ensure that you always know what's coming up and don't forget something big you have on your agenda.

What's even better about using an app like Google Calendar is that you can also let other people see your diary and contribute to it. This is a great way to arrange meetups and get-togethers because it lets people see when you're free.

Now comes one of the very biggest tips for organizing your life and getting things in order: make sure that you also add your other tasks and to-do list to your diary. Ask yourself what the things are that you absolutely can't miss. For instance, you might decide that at all costs you are going to go to the gym three times a week. Maybe you absolutely can't put off filling out your tax return any longer. So make sure it's in the diary and treat it just as you would any other activity – as immutable. If someone suggests doing something on that day and you have 'fill out tax return' already on that date, then you explain that you can't meet up, or that you'll have to get there a couple of hours later. It seems extreme but once you start taking your commitments seriously, you'll find you have much more time to do the things you want to do and that you don't feel stressed because those necessary tasks are constantly being pushed back.

Facebook

Facebook is one of the biggest culprits for many of us when it comes to procrastination, stress and overwhelm. Not only does Facebook take up a huge amount of time by giving us something to randomly browse through, but it can also lead to stress (and even depression) through something called 'social comparison theory' (we essentially compare our lives to the highlights that everyone else shows off). Then there's the fact that Facebook keeps us in touch with all those people we no longer know, no longer care about and no longer need to be in touch with.

So, what's the solution? You might expect me to say 'delete Facebook' at this point, but that would be rather rash – after all, Facebook is a very useful tool and can make organizing events and things a lot easier. Instead, simply take a look at your Facebook and streamline and prune it.

Firstly: you probably don't need the Facebook app on your phone! Not only does the Facebook app take up a lot of juice thereby draining your battery and slowing down your device but it can also constantly pester you with notifications and messages that aren't all that pressing. They come through as emails anyway, so why not turn off the app? More important is simply to delete those contacts on Facebook that aren't friends. People from your infant school, people whom you met at random parties and people whom you don't like can all go. And as for your news feed, why not just 'unfollow' some of the people you don't want to see?

Doing all these things will allow you to make more use of Facebook without the stressful/distracting/time-consuming elements. Then just make sure to limit your own Facebook use. For example, how about limiting yourself to 10 minutes of Facebook a day?

CHAPTER FOUR

Organising Your Time

In the last chapter, we looked at how to organise and optimize your social life. Some of this also relates more broadly to organizing your time. For instance, scheduling important tasks and things you want or need to do as though they were social commitments is a good example of how you can organise your time. But there's so much more to it than that.

Let's look at some of the things you can do to organise your time a little more easily.

Recognize Your Limits

The first and absolute most important point to consider when organizing your time is that you must consider your limitations. This is where a lot of us go wrong because we forget that our energy is finite as well as our time. A perfect example of getting this wrong is if you write yourself a new training program and diet. Often, we come up with plans to lose weight that essentially involve working out for an additional 3 hours on top of our regular training routines while also dieting.

So, you now have less energy and you're expected to start exerting yourself for a total of three hours, as well as travelling to and from the gym? This just doesn't work. If you find that you currently aren't doing all the things you would like to be doing, then once again you need to prioritize. Do you find out that you're not as healthy as you'd like to be? Then maybe it's time to stop going to the pub with your friends once a week. And you have never been able to get on top of the housework? Then maybe you need to quit that karate class!

Walk or Sit, Don't Wobble!

Likewise, you need to make sure that you always give yourself time to recover. We are much more productive when we have been given some time to recover and recharge our batteries. If you are just constantly doing one thing after another, then eventually you'll become tired and you'll stop working properly.

The heading of this section is an old saying that is particularly relevant to this discussion. 'Walk or Sit, Don't Wobble' basically means that you need to divide your time between resting and working. This prevents you from getting into those situations where you are 'half working'. Half working is the worst thing because it means that you aren't getting much done but you aren't relaxing either. Just as bad is 'half relaxing'.

Half relaxing is what you do when you're too tired to do anything useful, but you feel like you can't justify putting on a film, reading a book or taking a bath. So instead, you just sit there, watching rubbish TV. At the end of the day, you've achieved nothing, but you've also failed to enjoy the time off. This is why you need to allow yourself that recovery time and then make full use of it. Better yet, schedule it in and that way, you'll be able to look forward to it while you're working.

Timing Your Tasks

As you decide when to schedule those important tasks and when to schedule rest, it's useful to consider the natural ebbs and flows of your energy. All of us have times of day when we are more productive and times of day when we crash. Most of us for instance will find we crash when getting in from work and that we're less productive at work after 4 PM. Likewise, it takes us a little while to get around to being productive. Also important to consider is the way our other activities impact our energy levels. One of the easiest ways to make yourself exhausted and want to crash for instance is to eat dinner! Once you've eaten, your body needs to digest and that leaves you with little energy to do anything else. So instead of making dinner, eating on the sofa, and then planning on tidying, the tidying should always come before the eating.

Don't sit on the couch if you want to keep your energy levels up and don't eat until you've completed at least your most important task. You can always enjoy a light snack when you get in if you're too hungry to do anything!

Multitasking

In the chapter on work, we're going to talk about how multitasking can be a bad thing. However, in the right circumstances, multitasking can be highly useful. Multitasking at work doesn't usually work but in your private life, it can be useful in any situation where one of the tasks doesn't require your full attention. For instance, if you need to go shopping, you can call a friend on your hands-free kit while you're shopping. This way, you're able to catch up with your correspondence while at the same time getting in the food – two birds killed with one stone!

Likewise, you can sort out bills while washing up, or you can research activities on a tablet while cooking. This can help you to accomplish twice as much in a lot of circumstances so start looking for opportunities to tick off more than one of your tasks at once!

Close Open Loops

One very important tip to helping you feel more on top of life is to close all those smaller and fiddly tasks that you consider 'open loops'. In the next chapter, we'll see that it makes sense to work on the biggest and hardest task first so that you can ensure maximum productivity. At home though, you should aim to do the reverse. Tasks are generally less pressing at home, so it makes sense to tick off the smaller things you have to do so that you have less stress and fewer things weighing on your mind. This means things like paying that bill, things like calling that friend, things like RSVPing to that event. We put off these jobs because we find them stressful and don't want to use up energy thinking about them. As a result, we just end up worrying about them unconsciously and having less time and energy available to do anything else.

If you have something you can complete quickly that's playing on your mind then just tell yourself: it needs to be done eventually, so it's better to get it out of the way. Every day when you come home from work, give yourself half an hour to close off those 'open loops' so you have a small unconscious 'to-do' list.

CHAPTER FIVE

Work, Work, Work

If you've taken all of the above advice on board and started putting some of these systems in place, you should start to notice your life becoming a bit easier. You have more time, you have fewer decisions to make and you're less stressed thanks to a quieter social calendar. But you're probably still overworked and over-stressed and this comes down a lot of the time to your work. Work is what makes many of us so stressed and it's what leaves us with so little time to do anything else. Time to put a stop to that.

Be More Productive at Work

The first thing you need to do is to start approaching your work more productively and efficiently. How do you make sure that you get through that to-do list and that you aren't constantly treading water? The first thing you need to do is to remove multitasking from the equation.

While multitasking was useful in the last chapter, studies show that it simply doesn't work in a workplace environment. The simple reason for this is that activities that require our mental faculties don't enable multitasking. What you think is multitasking is sequential tasking – you're quickly switching from one task to another and back. This takes up more mental energy and less work gets done overall. Instead, then, you need to set out the tasks you need to do and then work through them in order until they're all complete. This means that you should start your day with a to-do list. And there's a definite art to coming up with a to-do list. Tim Ferriss, the author of the Four Hour Workweek, always talks about having one task that he absolutely must get completed that day and then completing that. Everything else, he considers to be 'extra'. This is generally the best attitude to take to any list of objectives. Complete the biggest and most important tasks first and then move on to the smaller ones. The reason this is so important is that the biggest task is going to take the most time, the most focus and the most energy. It's also going to give you the biggest sense of satisfaction once ticked off.

If you complete all the smaller tasks first, then you risk taking up a lot of time with switching between tasks, answering emails and setting things up. This can end up taking longer than you think and then not leaving enough time to complete that one 'big task' that you needed to finish. As a result, the day ends and you're left feeling stressed. Instead, work on that one massive task that will make a real difference first. Then start on those smaller jobs and get as many as possible out of the way. You can do this after 4 PM, at the point in the day when you're starting to feel less productive.

Removing Distractions

Now you have just one big task to complete during your work day, you should stand a much better chance of getting into a 'flow state'. A flow state is an almost mythical state of mind that is described by many productivity gurus. The idea is that by focusing on one job that you need to complete you can eventually get into a state of mind where you're able to shut out all outside distractions and work in a fast and focused manner. This results in the best work and also allows you to get through the task without procrastinating.

The most important key to being able to get into a state of flow is to make sure you remove distractions and things that can break your concentration. And the number one culprit? Email. Email at work is one of the things that is most responsible for causing us to become distracted and stressed and as soon as we start responding to emails we can find ourselves getting into a 'reactive' mindset as opposed to a 'proactive' one. Now we're working to someone else's agenda instead of our own and that means we're less likely to complete the tasks we set for ourselves.

One important tip then is to make sure that you complete at least a certain amount of work before you even look at your emails. You should aim to set yourself a certain amount of work before you complete any other task. How you might have previously started your day is by going and making a cup of tea, having a chat and answering your emails. By the time you've started completing any actual work, it's already 11 AM! So instead, start your day by sitting down and making a 'gentle start' on that one big project. Now set yourself a goal. If you have to write 6,000 words today for instance, then tell yourself you won't make that first cup of tea until you've completed 2,000 words. And you won't look at emails until you're on 5,000 words.

Suddenly, you've changed your regime to put the pressing work first. The psychological impact of having this much work 'under your belt' cannot be understated and because you have made such a start, you'll find it's much easier to just jump back into work. By the time you've answered those emails, you'll now have completed a huge amount of work and be well on top of your daily tasks!

Meanwhile, having a 'goal' to work to can act as great motivation.

The Pomodoro Technique

The Pomodoro Technique is another tool you can use to formalize this process. Simply use a timer and set yourself a specific amount of time that you're going to focus on your work. This can be 10 minutes, 20 minutes, or 60 minutes. Work until that time is complete and the timer sounds, and once that's happened, set the timer for 5 minutes to rest and relax.

Then, set the timer for another block of work. Dividing your day into periods of work and rest like this helps you to maintain separation between your productivity and recovery and this can prevent burnout while also helping you to finish more work.

Reducing Email

The only downside to this plan is that a lot of people will feel very unsure about ignoring their emails in case they are missing something very important. A way to avoid this nagging concern is to consider investing in a smartwatch. While you might think that having yet another device with notifications is only going to make matters worse this gives you a handy (no pun intended) way to check what the email is about without having to actually load up Gmail and potentially get sucked in.

Another option is to set up an autoresponder on your email that tells your audience you will only answer emails at certain times of day but that they can contact you by phone only if it's an emergency. When you do this, you ensure that there's always a way you can be reached in a serious emergency but at the same time, you also avoid getting inundated with unnecessary calls.

Reducing Communication Overhead

Communication overhead is a term used to describe the negative impact that lots of meetings, emails and phone calls can have on your productivity. When you're in a meeting you aren't working and when you're on the phone, you're not working! To get around this, try to keep unnecessary communication to an absolute minimum. You can reduce this in several different ways. For instance, if you find yourself in lots of long phone calls, consider asking people to email instead of calling. Alternatively, preface your phone calls by telling the person you're speaking to that you only have five minutes so you'll need to get straight to business. They may offer to call back but simply say 'no it's okay, but we'll just have to make it quick'.

As for meetings, consider discussing with your manager whether you need to be present for meetings. Try skipping one, to begin with, and explain that you have lots of work to finish and that you feel your time could be put to better use in other ways.

Flexitime

If you can arrange flexi-time with your work – or even arrange to work from home – then this can help you to save a huge amount of time on commuting and getting started with work. Again, try to discuss with your boss how you could be put to better use by doing other things with your time and you can provide the same service from home. The only real legitimate reason a company might need you to stay at the office is if you're needed to answer the switchboard. Otherwise, it will just be a matter of convincing them to let you give it a try – and then you prove yourself by completing even more work than you would do in the office.

Flexi-time meanwhile could just mean asking if you can come into work an hour earlier and leave an hour later.

This can make a huge difference if it helps you to avoid the rush hour and mean you save at least half an hour of your day... The point is that you don't have to work in the same manner as everyone else and it may be that other more effective work styles are better suited to your lifestyle. It just takes the confidence to push for the changes that suit you and to help your employer modernize a little!

CHAPTER SIX

Be Clear About Your Goals

One of the most important tools for organizing your time is to know your goals. When you know your goals, allows you to prioritize things a lot more easily. Know what's important to you, know where you're trying to get and know what you need to do to get there. This way, you can much more easily decide what is most pressing and what will help you get there. No one else can tell you what's important and what isn't. Not your employer, not your parents, not your partner. There is no 'right or wrong' way to live life, so you need to decide what's most important to you. Maybe that's your family, maybe it's your fitness, maybe it's becoming the next rock star sensation. It's all legitimate and it helps you to focus your life much more easily.

You may even decide that your goal in life is to have lots of friends and have lots of great adventures, memories, and experiences. In that case, you might decide to turn some of the advice in this book so far on its head. Maybe you spend less time at work and less time in the gym so that you have more time to fill your social calendar. Either way, you need to know where you're going and what's important to you.

This is a good place to start then. Instead of starting with a goal, start with a 'vision' and try to picture what you want your life to ideally look like. This should have much more of an emotional impact than simply writing down 'get rich'. What you might also find, is that once you start visualizing the lifestyle you want, it might impact what your goals are. For example, you might think you want to get rich – but if your vision is mostly about living in a beautiful home, or travelling a lot, then maybe the money is just a means to an end. Maybe your real goal is to have a better home or to travel more. And maybe there are better ways to accomplish those things!

Another popular tip is to imagine writing your eulogy. The point is to imagine that you have died and you're writing the speech you would like to be given at your funeral. In other words, how do you want to be remembered? Do you talk about what a family man you were? Or about how you had a life filled with adventures?

How to Write Goals Properly

Now you know what you want from life, the next step is to formalize that into useful and workable goals. The key here is not to make vague or useless goals. If your goal is: 'lose 10lbs by next year' then you are unlikely to be successful. Why? Because a year is a long time from now for starters. This means you can easily put things off and hope that you'll be able to get back on track later.

Another problem with writing goals like this is that a lot of it is outside of your control. In other words, even if you do everything right, you might not lose 10 lbs. This can be very disheartening and can lead to you losing motivation. So instead, your goals need to be concrete, short-term, and well within your control.

CHAPTER SEVEN

Limit Your Sources of Information

Things are hopefully starting to become a lot more simplified, streamlined and organised for you at this point and you should have a much better handle on all the tasks you need to complete. But there are still some sources of concern – which include all those things that keep distracting you and trying to rob you of your focus. And in particular, one of the biggest culprits is all those 'screens'. All the information and stimulation coming from the TV, the smartphone, the laptop, and more are constantly keeping us 'wired' and stressed.

We're on constant alert for messages (so much so that we feel 'phantom vibrations' in our pockets sometimes!) and we can hardly go more than five minutes without feeling the need to load up some form of technology. This isn't healthy and it's certainly not conducive to productivity. So, what do you do? Here are some ways to limit all that information and data coming in.

Pick Some New Hobbies

For many of us, every hobby that we have involves a screen of some sort – whether it's gaming, watching films or using the computer. There's nothing wrong with this per se, but it sure can stress you out over time and lead to burnout if it's all you're doing to relax. To avoid this situation then, make sure that you have some hobbies in your life that don't involve screens and that require sustained focus and attention. A good example of that would be reading. Reading a book not only offers a reprieve from the screen but also means that you need to stay focused on that one thing for a good amount of time. Instead of flitting from one information stream to the next, your mind is completely focused and relaxed. This is almost like meditation.

Another good example is drawing. Drawing is a very relaxing hobby and you'd be surprised just how much pressure it can take off you and how time flies when you're enjoying it. And you don't even need to be 'good' necessarily. Going to the gym or playing sports is also good and so are things like DIY, bird watching, walking... anything where your phone stays in your pocket. And then make sure that you abide by this rule and keep your phone away for this duration. Again, if you're worried about missing something important then consider using a smartwatch. Or perhaps just setting ringtones for priority callers.

Meditation

Perhaps the most meditative hobby you can take up though is meditation! Meditation is simply the act of taking control of your inner monologue and using it to bring your mind to calm. Different forms of meditation work differently – mindfulness vs. transcendental for instance – but they both offer the same benefits.

Not only is meditation shown to be very good for us in the short term by helping to encourage slower brain waves, but it also provides tools for combating stress and staying focused as necessary.

Have Quiet Time

The point at which your phones and computers become most destructive is in the evening. Not only do screens stress us out but the light itself also causes the release of cortisol – which acts against the release of melatonin. In other words, our brain treats a phone screen just like natural sunlight ad prevents us from getting into a sleeping state of mind.

There are many solutions to this – some of which get quite ridiculous and include things like wearing blue-blocking shades to bed. Though, the most effective way to avoid light from screens before bed is simply to stop using computers and phones for at least an hour before you go to sleep. Let your friends know that you'll be doing this, or even consider setting up an auto text response that is triggered after this time (Android apps like Tasker can help you do this).

And better yet, use half an hour to read a book or something before you doze off. This will quiet your mind and help you to get deeper sleep once you do hit the hay. And hopefully, it should go without saying that when you get home at the end of the day and are off work you do not answer any emails that are related to work. Don't even look at your work email – it will only prevent you from properly relaxing and enjoying your time off!

CHAPTER EIGHT

Value Your Time

Successful entrepreneurs aren't 'yes' men or women. These are people who value their time and who want to invest that time wisely. Whether you're an entrepreneur or not, try to take the same approach. Your time is the most asset you have and eventually, it will run out. Don't waste it working on projects you don't care about, spending time with people you don't like or completing work for other people. Guard it fiercely and only use it in ways that are conducive to helping you get what YOU want out of life.

This is why it was so important for us to set our goals in chapter 6. And it's why it's so important to prune your social calendar and to learn to say 'no' more. But it should also change the way you think about your time. Every decision you make ultimately comes down to the best way to utilize your time. When you get a text from a friend at work, you have to decide whether it's worth answering now or trying to get that little bit more work done.

Most of us trade our time for money in our careers. This essentially means that you're valuing your time at that amount. When you think about this and when you think about how little time you have to do the things you love, then hopefully this will motivate you to go out there and chase what you are worth. And hopefully, it will make you realize that you should fight for all the free time you have around your work – whether that means your commute, just trying to organise flexi-time or the chance to work from home.

Outsourcing

It also means that you should think differently about the way you're spending your money. If spending money means you can buy back more time, then this will very often be a very good use of your money. That might mean outsourcing work such as cleaning to a cleaner, or it might mean getting a dishwasher. There are many other ways you can outsource your tasks too and get more time back. For example, consider hiring a 'virtual assistant'. These are people who will complete any task for you that can be completed remotely.

In other words, the service operates only by email and over the phone, which means that they can handle things for you like making appointments, arranging meetings, doing research and answering emails. Traditionally, virtual assistants are used by entrepreneurs and small businesses. However, they can also be used for a range of personal tasks whether that means booking a table at a restaurant, researching your next car or suggesting holidays! The best bit about virtual assistants is that they tend to be incredibly affordable: often they will charge as little as $3 for an hour of work. The limitation, other than the fact that they must work remotely, is that you will normally be outsourcing to India. This means that they may not be native English speakers – so they might not be candidates to finish that report or essay for you. There are many other ways to outsource your work too. Just understand that this can be a great way to invest your money and think of it as buying time.

CHAPTER NINE

Be Vocal

There's another way to outsource jobs that you can't complete on your own and to get help as well. And what is that? Simple: ask your friends for help! A lot of us feel bad about asking for help because we don't want to be a burden and/or show weakness. The reality though, is that friends are there to help each other and this cuts both ways. If you are struggling with the large number of tasks you have and you're feeling overwhelmed and stressed, chances are that your friends will want to help you.

Asking Friends for Help

There are many examples of tasks that can be made a little easier with some help from your friends. Perhaps you're moving home for example. Instead of spending all your time and energy moving your things yourself, consider asking a friend if they'll help you organise your possessions and transport them with you.

Meanwhile, if you find you don't have time to look for holiday ideas, why not just ask your friends if they have any good recommendations? And if you're struggling and you don't have time to pick up your children from school, then why not ask another parent if they can help?

Often you can share the burden with friends as a way to reduce your workload too. Why not take it in turns to pick up your kids from work for example that way you'll have to spend almost 50% less time driving to and from school! Likewise, you could even agree to do a similar system for the weekly shop.

Of course, you don't want to take advantage of your friends and keep getting them to do things for you. But when you're struggling, there is nothing wrong with just asking for a little help – you'd do the same for them! And when it's mutually beneficial, then there's no downside!

Other Ways to be Vocal

Being vocal doesn't just mean asking your friends for help though. Sometimes it can also mean doing the opposite. Sometimes you might find yourself doing too much for your friends or shouldering too much of the work and chores at home. In either of these situations, being vocal might just mean speaking up and telling your friends, family, or partner that you're going to have to start doing a little less.

This is even more important at work. If you find that you keep getting more and more work piled on, this can be highly disheartening – especially if it feels like you're carrying other people. Don't be afraid to speak up and tell your employer that you have too much work and that you're struggling – or even to outright refuse to take on anyone else's work unless it's reflected in your salary. This all comes back to what we were talking about in the last chapter: valuing your time!

CHAPTER TEN

Health Habits to Adopt

So that's it: that's everything you need to know to start organizing your time better, getting help where you need it and valuing your time. Decide what you really want to spend your time doing and how you want to spend your life and then just prioritize that above everything else. What's left is to give yourself the best fighting chance of success possible. And the way we're going to do that is by helping you to strengthen your body and mind ready to take on that work schedule and emerge on top!

Eating for Energy

We discussed earlier that energy and not time, was the most valuable commodity when it comes to getting everything done and thereby having more freedom later. We talked about how you could give yourself more energy by implementing breaks and rests and by working with your natural rhythms. But what's also important is to provide your body with energy throughout the day.

So how do you eat for energy? One tip is to try and get more complex carbohydrates and fats. Complex carbohydrates are carbs like vegetables and wholegrain bread that are slower to digest. These release energy slowly throughout the day – as does fat – and that in turn means you avoid having a 'sugar high' followed by a crash. Avoid sweets and cakes because these are 'simple carbs' that release a rush of sugar and then leave you feeling tired and low on energy subsequently.

Equally important is to ensure you are getting all your vitamins and minerals. These are crucial elements in our diet that lead to greater energy and greater function throughout our bodies. Vitamins and minerals improve everything from our mood (by contributing to the creation of hormones and neurotransmitters), to our sleep, bone density, energy efficiency and more. Adding a smoothie to your daily diet can make a huge difference – and in this case, it's worth the sugar!

Clean, Sharp, and Impressive

Another tip is to invest in your hygiene and your style. The secret is to feel good and to look good. When you do this, you'll find it's much easier to stay positive, productive, and driven. Get your hair cut regularly, make the effort to wear sharp outfits that suit you and maintain good hygiene. When you feel clean on the inside, you'll express that on the outside. And when you feel confident in the way you look, you're giving off an aura of success that will lead to more opportunities.

More Lifestyle Tips

We've already addressed the value of meditation, and this is a great tool you can use to keep your mind relaxed. If you find that you struggle a lot with stress, then you should also think about addressing the sources of that stress, which may even mean quitting your job. You can also try seeing a therapist. Often the most effective form of therapy for stress is 'CBT' (cognitive behavioural therapy) which will help to teach you the mental tools and skills that can help you to eliminate unhelpful thoughts and anxieties.

Finally, if you can find the time and the energy, it is very much worth spending some time on a basic exercise regime. Even if your goal isn't to lose weight or build muscle, exercising will simply help to give you more energy and focus throughout the day. It acts as a natural depressant, improves the energy efficiency of your cells, and even helps you to get more energy to your brain. And it leads to better sleep!

Conclusion

You should now have all the tools and knowledge necessary to start organising your brain and your life and finally feel on top of things. It's a lot to take on board and of course, it's not going to change overnight. Try to avoid the temptation to force yourself to adopt all these changes right away – instead, take some time out to fix as much as you can and then try to slowly introduce as many positive new habits as you can.

If you're looking for an action plan you can follow, you can try the following.

A Day to Rearrange

First, take one day off to deal with as much as you can and thereby give yourself a good fighting chance. On this day, you're now going to do the following:

- Clean and tidy everything up.
- Invest in things that can help you stay on top of chores – like a handheld vacuum cleaner.
- Implement systems – such as washing up immediately after you've eaten, or keeping clothes to be ironed somewhere useful and out of the way.
- Complete your 'open loops' – the small niggling tasks that are causing you stress.
- Throw out lots of items to create less clutter.
- Define your goals.
- Prioritize social time with the people who are most important to you in life.

Moving Forward

From there on, try your best to follow these principles to help keep everything in order:

- Ask for help when you need it.
- Learn to say "no" when people invite you out and you just don't have time.
- Complete big tasks first at work.
- Make plans for the week to reduce decision fatigue.
- Add things you need to do to your diary and treat them just like your social plans – as non-negotiable.
- Look after your health and eat for energy.
- Schedule time off.
- Turn off screens an hour before bed.

At Work

- Negotiate flexitime with work or working from home.
- Work on large projects first.
- Reduce communication overhead.
- Avoid distractions.
- Value your time and make sure others do too.
- Ask for help if you need it.
- When you get home from work – switch it off!

Start putting this into practice, give it time and look for more ways that you can organise all the information coming in and give yourself more time.

Just remember that your happiness is the number one priority. If all the information and stress are doing anything to harm that, then something must change!

Organise your mind and your life and take back control of your time!

9 798889 862154

Printed by Libri Plureos GmbH in Hamburg, Germany